THE VOCAL LIBRARY

TENOR

Mozart Arias

Edited by
Robert L. Larsen and Richard Walters

To access companion recorded accompaniments online, visit:
www.halleonard.com/mylibrary

Enter Code
8075-3125-5405-6656

Aria Text Editor and Translator: Martha Gerhart
Assistant Editor: Janet Neis

On the cover, Nicolas Lancret, *La Camargo Dancing*, c. 1730, oil on canvas, 30 x42 inches,
Andrew W. Mellon Collection, © 1992 National Gallery of Art, Washington

ISBN 978-0-7935-6241-1

HAL•LEONARD®
CORPORATION
7777 W. BLUEMOUND RD. P.O. BOX 13819 MILWAUKEE, WI 53213

Visit Hal Leonard Online at
www.halleonard.com

CONTENTS

ROBERT L. LARSEN is the compiler and editor of the bestselling *G. Schirmer Opera Anthology,* in five volumes, and also collaborated with Evelyn Lear in recorded and published master classes, released by G. Schirmer in two volumes, *Lyric Soprano Arias: A Master Class with Evelyn Lear.* Dr. Larsen is featured as a pianist on a score/audio package of *Songs of Joseph Marx* from Hal Leonard Publishing, and is compiler of a series of opera scenes for study and workshop performances.

Dr. Larsen is founder and artistic director of one of America's major opera festivals, the critically acclaimed Des Moines Metro Opera, and since the company's founding in 1973 has served as conductor and stage director for all of its productions. Since 1965 Dr. Larsen has also been chairman of the department of music at Simpson College in Indianola, Iowa, and during his tenure the department has received national recognition and awards for its serious and extensive program of operatic training for undergraduates. He holds a bachelor's degree from Simpson College, a master's degree in piano performance from the University of Michigan, and a doctorate in opera and conducting from Indiana University. His piano studies were with Sven Lekberg, Joseph Brinkman, Rudolph Ganz, and Walter Bricht. Dr. Larsen is highly regarded as an opera coach and accompanist. He has coached singers at Tanglewood, Oglebay Park, West Virginia, Chicago, and New York, and has assisted in the training of many artists with significant operatic careers.

Dr. Larsen was the recipient of the first Governor's Award in Music presented by the Iowa Arts Council, and is listed in "Who's Who in America." In addition to his many other musical accomplishments, he is an avid student of the Renaissance, and specializes in bringing to life the great vocal works of that period.

MOZART ARIAS FOR TENOR

DIE ENTFÜHRUNG AUS DEM SERAIL
(The Abduction from the Seraglio)

The libretto is by Gottlieb Stephanie the Younger, adapted from *Belmont und Constanze* by Christoph Friedrich Bretzner (set to music by Johann André and premiered in Berlin in 1781). The opera was premiered at the Burgtheater in Vienna on July 16, 1782. The story is set at the country palace of the Pasha Selim in Turkey during the sixteenth century.

Hier soll ich dich denn sehen

from Act I
character: Belmonte

As the opera opens, Belmonte, a young Spanish nobleman, has been searching for his beloved Constanze, who has been captured by pirates. He arrives at the palace of the Pasha Selim, where he hopes to find Constanze.

Hier soll ich dich denn sehen,	*Here at last shall I see you,*
Constanze, dich, mein Glück!	*Constanze—you, my happiness!*
O Himmel, hör' mein Flehen:	*Oh heaven, hear my supplication:*
gieb mir die Ruh' zurück!	*restore peace to me!*
Ich duldete der Leiden, o Liebe, allzuviel.	*I have endured all too many sorrows, oh Love.*
Gieb mir dafür nun Freuden,	*Now grant me joys, instead,*
und bringe mich an's Ziel.	*and lead me to my goal.*

O wie ängstlich

from Act I
character: Belmonte

Belmonte has just learned that the captured Constanze is alive and is hoping to be rescued. He is elated, and anxiously imagines seeing his beloved again.

Constanze! Dich wiederzusehen—dich!	*Constanze! To see you again—you!*
O wie ängstlich, o wie feurig	*Oh how anxiously, oh how ardently*
klopft mein liebevolles Herz!	*beats my loving heart!*
Und des Wiedersehens Zähre	*And the tears of reunion*
lohnt der Trennung bangen Schmerz.	*will requite the anxious pain of separation.*
Schon zittr' ich und wanke;	*Already I tremble and shake;*
schon zag' ich und schwanke.	*already I waver and falter.*
Es hebt sich die schwellende Brust.	*My surging breast rises.*
Ist das ihr Lispeln?	*Is that her whisper?*
Es wird mir so bange.	*I am becoming uneasy.*
War das ihr Seufzen?	*Was that her sighing?*
Es glüht mir die Wange.	*My cheeks are glowing.*
Täuscht mich die Liebe?	*Is love deceiving me?*
War es ein Traum?	*Was it a dream?*

Frisch zum Kampfe!

from Act II
character: Pedrillo

Pedrillo is not really looking forward to the perils of the abduction. He enters with two bottles of wine and resolves to face the situation as bravely as possible.

Frisch zum Kampfe!	*Quick to the battle!*
Frisch zum Streite!	*Quick to the fight!*
Nur ein feiger Tropf verzagt.	*Only a cowardly fool refuses.*
Sollt' ich zittern?	*Should I tremble?*
Sollt' ich zagen?	*Should I hesitate?*
Nicht mein Leben muthig wagen?	*Not risk my life courageously?*
Nein. Ach nein, es sei gewagt!	*No. Ah, no, let it be risked!*

Ich baue ganz

from Act III
character: Belmonte

Belmonte and Pedrillo are about to abduct Constanze and Blonde from the palace. Belmonte looks forward to his reunion with Constanze and trusts the power of love to help him accomplish his mission.

Ich baue ganz auf deine Stärke,	*I rely entirely on your power,*
vertrau', o Liebe, deiner Macht;	*I trust, oh love, in your might;*
denn ach, was wurden nicht für Werke	*for, ah—what kind of deeds have not,*
schon oft durch dich zustand gebracht!	*after all, often been accomplished through you!*
Was aller Welt unmöglich scheint,	*That which to all the world seems impossible*
wird durch die Liebe doch vereint.	*will yet be reconciled through love.*

LE NOZZE DI FIGARO
(The Marriage of Figaro)

The libretto is by Lorenzo da Ponte, based on the comedy *La Folle Journée, ou Le Mariage de Figaro* by Pierre-Auguste Caron de Beaumarchais. The play was premiered in Paris in 1784; the opera was premiered at the Burgtheater in Vienna on May 1, 1786. The story is set at the palace of Count Almaviva, near Seville, in the seventeenth century (usually played as the eighteenth century).

In quegli anni

from Act IV
character: Basilio

Figaro, valet to Count Almaviva, has discovered that his bride Susanna has agreed to a rendezvous with the Count on their wedding night. He asks Bartolo and Basilio to hide with him so that when the Count and Susanna meet, the three can jump out and surprise the pair. Basilio, a music master, tells Bartolo that he was once a daring young man like Figaro, but he soon learned that to get ahead it's best to flatter the rich and powerful.

In quegli anni, in cui val poco	During those years in which practical
la mal pratica ragion,	reasoning doesn't count for much,
ebbi anch'io lo stesso foco,	I, too, had the same impetuosity;
fui quel pazzo, ch'or non son.	I was such a fool, which I am not, now.
Che col tempo e coi perigli,	For with time and tribulations,
Donna Flemma capitò;	"Lady Phlegm" presented herself;
e i capricci ed i puntigli	and she drove the whims and punctilios
dalla testa mi cavò.	out of my head.
Presso un picciolo abituro,	To a humble little dwelling
seco lei mi trasse un giorno,	she took me with her one day;
e togliendo giù dal muro	and, taking down from the wall
del pacifico soggiorno	of the peaceful abode
una pelle di somaro,	a donkey's pelt,
«Prendi,» disse, «o figlio caro!»	"Take it," she said, "oh dear son!"
Poi disparve, e mi lasciò.	Then she disappeared, and left me.
Mentre ancor tacito guardo quel dono,	While I'm still gazing, speechless, at that gift,
il ciel s'annuvola,	the sky becomes cloudy—
rimbomba il tuono,	it thunders—
mista alla grandine	mixed with hailstones,
scroscia la piova.	down pours the rain.
Ecco le membra coprir mi giova	So, it's useful to cover my limbs
col manto d'asino, che mi donò.	with the cloak of ass which she gave me.
Finisce il turbine; nè fo due passi,	The squall ends; I take but two steps
che fiera orribile dinanzi a me fassi.	when a horrible wild beast comes before me.
Già mi tocca l'ingorda bocca,	Already the greedy mouth touches me;
già di difendermi speme non ho.	I have no hope of defending myself.
Ma il fiuto ignobile del mio vestito	But the ignoble smell of my garment
tolse alla belva sì l'appetito,	so took away the appetite of the beast
che disprezzandomi, si rinselvò.	that, scorning me, he went back into the forest.
Così conoscere mi fè la sorte,	Thus did fate make me learn
ch'onte, pericoli, vergogna, e morte,	that infamies, dangers, shame, and death
col cuojo d'asino fuggir si può.	can be avoided with the hide of an ass.

DON GIOVANNI

The libretto is by Lorenzo da Ponte, after Giovanni Bertati's libretto for Giuseppe Gazzaniga's opera *Il convitato di pietra;* also after the Don Juan legends. *Don Giovanni* was premiered at the National Theater in Prague on October 29, 1787. The story is set in and near Seville during the seventeenth century (usually played as the eighteenth century).

Dalla sua pace

from Act I
character: Don Ottavio

Donna Anna seems sure that Don Giovanni has been responsible for the attack on her person as well as the murder of her father. In this aria, written to replace "Il mio tesoro" in the Vienna production of 1788, Ottavio insists that he will know peace only when his fiancée's tranquility is assured.

Come mai creder deggio	How should I ever believe
di sì nero delitto capace un cavaliere!	a gentleman capable of such a heinous crime?
Ah, di scoprire il vero	Ah, to discover the truth
ogni mezzo si cerchi.	may every means be sought.
Io sento in petto	I hear within the breast
e di sposo e d'amico	of both husband and friend
il dover che mi parla:	the duty that speaks to me:
disingannarla voglio, o vendicarla!	I will disabuse her, or avenge her!

Dalla sua pace la mia dipende.	*My peace depends on hers.*
Quel che a lei piace	*That which pleases her*
vita mi rende;	*gives me life;*
quel che le incresce	*that which displeases her*
morte mi dà.	*kills me.*
S'ella sospira, sospiro anch'io.	*If she sighs, I sigh too.*
È mia quell'ira;	*That rage is mine;*
quel pianto è mio,	*that mourning is mine,*
e non ho bene s'ella non l'ha.	*and I do not have joy if she doesn't.*

Il mio tesoro

from Act II

character: Don Ottavio

At last Don Ottavio is convinced that Don Giovanni is responsible for the murder of Donna Anna's father. He declares his determination to avenge this wrong and to bring comfort to his beloved.

Il mio tesoro intanto andate a consolar,	*Go, meanwhile, to console my beloved;*
e del bel ciglio il pianto cercate di asciugar.	*and try to dry the tears from her beautiful eyes.*
Ditele che i suoi torti a vendicar io vado:	*Tell her that I am going off to avenge her wrongs...*
che sol di stragi e morti nunzio vogl'io tornar, sì!	*that I will come back messenger only of ravages and deaths—yes!*

COSÌ FAN TUTTE
(Women Are Like That)

The libretto is an original story by Lorenzo da Ponte. The opera was premiered at the Burgtheater in Vienna on January 26, 1790. The story is set at the home of Fiordiligi and her sister Dorabella in Naples during the seventeenth century (most often played as the eighteenth century).

Un'aura amorosa

from Act I

character: Ferrando

Ferrando and Guglielmo, young Neapolitan soldiers, are disguised as Albanians, having consented to go along with a plot devised by their friend Don Alfonso to prove or disprove that their girlfriends can be tempted into faithlessness. Ferrando, after the first chapter in this deception, remains in the garden to reflect on the sustaining powers of love.

Un'aura amorosa del nostro tesoro	*A loving breath from our beloved*
un dolce ristoro al cor porgerà...	*will grant sweet solace to the heart...*
al cor che nudrito da speme d'amore,	*to the heart which, fed by hope of love,*
d'un esca migliore bisogno non ha.	*has no need for better nourishment.*

Ah! lo veggio quell'anima bella

from Act II
character: Ferrando

Disguised as an Albanian, Ferrando attempts to convince Fiordiligi that she cannot resist his advances.

Non sperarlo se pria gli occhi
gli occhi men fieri me non giri.
O ciel, ma tu mi guardi,
e poi sospiri?

Don't hope for that unless you first
turn your eyes to me less haughtily.
But—oh heaven—you are looking at me
and then sighing?

Ah, lo veggio, quell'anima bella
al mio pianto resister non sa:
non è fatta per esser rubella
agli affetti di amica pietà.
In quel guardo, in quei cari sospiri
dolce raggio lampeggia al mio cor:
già rispondi a miei caldi desiri,
già tu cedi al più tenero amor.
Ma tu fuggi, spietata, tu taci,
ed invano mi senti languir?
Ah, cessate, speranze fallaci,
la crudel mi condanna a morir.

Ah, I see it: that beautiful soul
can not resist my tears;
it wasn't made to be rebellious
to feelings of friendly compassion.
At that gaze, at those dear sighs,
a sweet ray of hope lights up my heart:
you are already responding to my warm desires;
you are already yielding to the tenderest love.
But you flee, merciless woman—you are silent,
and you hear me lament in vain?
Ah, cease, false hopes;
the cruel woman condemns me to die.

DIE ZAUBERFLÖTE
(The Magic Flute)

The libretto is by Emanuel Schikaneder, based on a fairy tale from the collection *Dschinnistan* by Christoph Martin Wieland (three volumes, published in Weimar beginning in 1786). The *Singspiel* was premiered at the Theater auf der Wieden in Vienna on September 30, 1791. The story is set in legendary, ancient Egypt.

Dies Bildnis ist bezaubernd schön

from Act I
character: Tamino

The prince Tamino has just been saved from the jaws of a mighty serpent by three ladies from the court of the Queen of the Night. They give him a portrait of the daughter of the queen. He reflects on her beauty and the new emotions that it inspires in him.

Dies Bildnis ist bezaubernd schön,
wie noch kein Auge je gesehn!
Ich fühl' es, wie dies Götterbild
mein Herz mit neuer Regung füllt.
Dies Etwas kann ich zwar nicht nennen;
doch fühl ich's hier wie Feuer brennen.
Soll die Empfindung Liebe sein?
Ja, ja! Die Liebe ist's allein.
O wenn ich sie nur finden könnte!
O wenn sie doch schon vor mir stände!
Ich würde...warm und rein—
was würde ich?
Ich würde sie voll Entzükken
an diesen heißen Busen drücken,
und ewig wäre sie dann mein.

This portrait is enchantingly beautiful,
as no eye has ever before beheld!
I feel it—how this godlike image
fills my heart with new emotion.
I cannot really name this thing;
yet I feel it here, burning like fire.
Could this sensation be love?
Yes, yes! It is love alone.
Oh, if only I could find her!
Oh, if only she were already here before me!
I would...warmly and chastely—
what would I?
I would, full of delight,
press her to this burning breast;
and then she would be forever mine.

Hier soll ich dich denn sehen

from
DIE ENTFÜHRUNG AUS DEM SERAIL

Andante

BELMONTE:

Hier soll ich dich denn

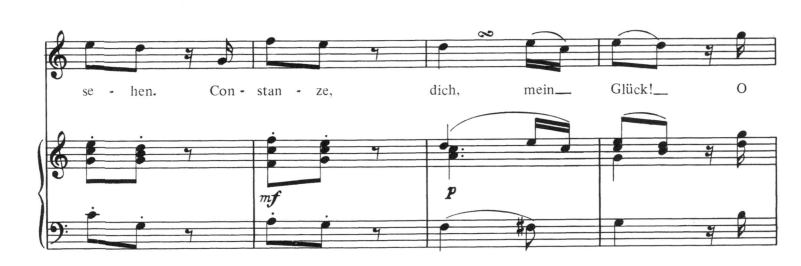

se - hen. Con - stan - ze, dich, mein__ Glück!__ O

Him - mel, hör' mein Fle - hen: gieb mir die Ruh' zu - rück gieb mir

die Ruh' zu - rück! Ich dul-de-te der Lei - den, o

Lie - be, ich dul-de-te der Lei - den, o Lie - be, o

Lie - be,_ all - zu - viel, all - zu - viel. Gieb mir da - für nun

- ge mich,_____ und brin - ge mich an's Ziel, und brin -

- ge mich,_____ und brin -

- ge mich an's Ziel.

O wie ängstlich

from
DIE ENTFÜHRUNG AUS DEM SERAIL

Recit.
BELMONTE:

Con - stan - ze! Con - stan - ze! Dich wie - der - zu -

sotto voce   dolce

*   Andante

se - hen— dich!   O wie ängst-lich, o wie feu - rig

sf   p   p   f

klopft mein lie - be - vol - les Herz,___ klopft mein

pp

* Appoggiatura possible

lie - be - vol - les Herz,— klopft mein lie - be -

sf *p*

vol - - - - - - - les

Herz! Und_ des_ Wie - der - se - hens_

f *p*

Zäh - re lohnt_ der_ Tren - nung_ bang - en—

f *p*

Schmerz, lohnt___ der___ Tren - nung___

ban - gen___ Schmerz. Schon zittr' ich und

wan-ke; schon zag' ich und schwan - ke, schon zag'___ ich und

schwan - ke.

pp

Es hebt sich die schwel - len - de

Brust,

cresc.

es hebt sich die schwel - len - de

Brust,

es hebt sich die schwel - len - de Brust.

f

pp

Ist das ihr Lis - peln? Es wird mir so—

p

ban - ge.

War das ihr Seuf - zen? Es glüht mir die—

Wan - ge. Täuscht mich die Lie - be? War es ein

Traum? Täuscht mich die Lie - be? War es ein

Traum? Täuscht mich die Lie - be? War es ein

Traum? O wie ängst - lich, o wie feu - rig

klopft mein lie - be - vol - les Herz,— klopft mein

lie - be-vol - les Herz, klopft mein lie - be -

vol - - - - les

Herz! Ist das ihr

Lis - peln? War das ihr

Seuf - zen? Es wird— mir so ban - ge. Es glüht— mir die

Wan - ge, es glüht mir die Wan - ge. O wie ängst - lich, o— wie

feu - rig klopft mein lie - be-vol - les Herz,—

klopft mein lie - be-vol - les— Herz,— klopft— mein—

24

lie - be - vol - les— Herz! Schon zittr' ich und

wan - ke; schon zag' ich und schwan - ke. O wie

ängst - lich, o— wie feu - rig klopft mein lie - be - vol - les

Herz,— klopft mein— lie - be - vol - les— Herz,—

klopft____ mein__ lie - be - vol - les__ Herz, mein__

lie - be - vol - les__ Herz, mein__ lie - be - vol - les__

Herz!

Frisch zum Kampfe!

from
DIE ENTFÜHRUNG AUS DEM SERAIL

PEDRILLO:

Frisch   zum

Kam - pfe!   Frisch   zum   Strei - te!

Nur ein___ fei - ger Tropf ver - zagt, nur ein

fei - ger Tropf ver - zagt. Sollt' ich

zit - tern? Sollt' ich za - gen? Nicht mein

Le - ben mu - thig wa - gen, nicht mein Le - ben mu - thig

Le - ben mu - thig wa - gen, nicht mein Le - ben mu - thig

wa - gen?

Nein. Ach nein, es sei ge - wagt! Ach

nein,nein,nein, es sei ge - wagt. Nein,_____ es sei ge-

Kam - pfe! Frisch zum Strei - te! Frisch, frisch zum

Kam - pfe! Frisch zum Strei - te! Frisch zum Kam - pfe!

Frisch zum Strei - te!

Nur ein— fei - ger Tropf ver - zagt, nur ein fei - ger Tropf ver -

zagt. Frisch zum Kam - pfe! Frisch zum Kam - pfe! Frisch zum Strei - te!

f

Ich baue ganz

from
DIE ENTFÜHRUNG AUS DEM SERAIL

BELMONTE:

Ich bau - e _ ganz _ auf _ dei - ne Stär - ke, ver -

trau', _ o _ Lie - be, _ dei - ner _ Macht, _ ver - trau', _ o _

Lie - be, o Lie - be, _ dei - ner Macht;

denn ach, was wur-den nicht für Wer - ke schon

oft durch dich___ zu-stand ge-bracht, was wur - den_nicht für

Wer-ke schon oft___ durch_dich zu-stand ge - bracht!

Was al - ler Welt_ un_ mög - lich_scheint, wird durch die Lie - be_

doch ver-eint, wird durch die Lie - be durch die Lie - be_ doch ver-

eint,_____ wird durch die Lie - be, durch die Lie - be_doch ver -

eint,_____

_____ doch ver - eint,_____ doch_ver -

eint,_____ doch_ver - eint.

Was al - ler Welt un - mög - lich_ scheint, wird durch die Lie - be

doch_ ver - eint,

was al - ler __

Welt, al - ler Welt __ unmög - lich scheint, wird durch __ die __

Lie - be, durch die Lie - be __ doch __ ver - eint. __

Ich bau - e __ ganz __ auf __

dei - ne Stär - ke, ver - trau', _____ o _____ Lie - be, dei - ner _____

Macht, _____ ver - trau', _____ o _____ Lie - be, o Lie - be, _____

dei - ner Macht; denn

ach, was wur - den _ nicht für Wer - ke schon oft durch _

dich___ zu-stand ge - bracht,   schon oft ____ durch__ dich   zu- stand ge -

bracht,_____

_p_

schon__ oft,__ schon__

oft_ durch_dich_zu - stand____ ge - bracht! Was

al - ler Welt_un - mög - lich_scheint, wird durch die Lie-be___ doch ver-eint

wird durch die Lie - be, durch die Lie - be___ doch ver - eint,_____

wird durch die Lie - be, durch die Lie - be___ doch ver - eint,_____

fp

wird durch die Lie - be __ doch __ ver -

eint. __

doch __ ver - eint, __ doch __ ver - eint, __ doch __ ver -

eint.

In quegli anni

from
LE NOZZE DI FIGARO

paz - zo, ch'or non son, fui quel paz - zo, ch'or non son. Che col

tem - po e coi pe - ri - gli, Don-na Flem-ma ca - pi - tò; e i ca -

pri - ci ed i pun - ti - gli dal - la te - sta mi ca -

vò, dal - la te - sta mi ca - vò.

Pres-so un pic-cio-lo a-bi - tu-ro, se-co lei mi tras - se un

gior - no, e to-glien-do giù dal mu - ro del pa-ci - fi - co sog -

cresc. p cresc.

gior - no u - na pel le di so - ma - ro, di so-ma-ro, di-so -

p cresc. p cresc. f

ma - ro. «Pren - di,» dis - se, «o fi - glio ca - ro,»

p

nu - vo-la, rim - bom - ba il tuo - no, mi-sta al-la

gran - di - ne scro -scia la pio - va, scro-scia la pio - va.

Ec - co le mem - bra co - prir mi gio - va col man - to

d'a - si-no, che mi do - nò, col man - to d'a - si - no,

che mi do - nò. Fi - ni-sce il tur - bi - ne, ne fo due pas - si,

che fie - ra or - ri - bi-le dian - zi a me fas - si;

Già, già mi toc - ca l'in - gor - da

boc - ca, già di di - fen-der-mi spe - me non ho,

speme non ho, speme non ho. Ma il fiuto i-

gno - bi - le del mio ve - sti - to tol - se al - la bel - va

si l'ap - pe - ti - to, che di - sprez - zan - do - mi, che di - sprez - zan - do - mi,

si rin - sel - vò, si rin - sel-

gir si può, col cuo - io d'a - si - no fug - gir si può, col cuo - io

d'a - si - no fug - gir si può, fug - gir si

può, fug - gir si può.

cresc.

Dalla sua pace

from
DON GIOVANNI

*Appoggiatura recommended

Andantino sostenuto

Dal - la sua pa - ce la mi-a di - pen - de.

Quel che_a lei pia - ce_ vi - ta mi_ ren - de;

quel che le_in - cre - sce mor - te mi dà, mor -

te, mor - te mi dà. S'el - la so -

spi - ra, so - spi - ro_an-ch'i - o. È mia quell'

i - ra; quel pian - to_è mi - o, e non ho_ be - ne

s'el - la non l'ha, e non_ho_ be - ne s'el - la non

l'ha, e non_ho_ be - ne s'el - la non l'ha.

Dal - la sua pa - ce la mi-a di - pen - de. Quel che a lei

pia - ce— vi - ta mi ren - de; quel che le in - cre - sce

cresc.

mf

mor - te mi dà, mor - te, mor - te mi

f

p *cresc.* *p*

dà. Dal - la sua pa - ce la mia di - pen - de. Quel che a lei pia - ce vi - ta mi

ren - de;_____ quel che le in - cre - sce mor - te mi dà,

mor - - te, mor - te mi dà,

mor - te mi dà, quel che le in - cre - sce_____ mor - te mi dà.

Il mio tesoro

from
DON GIOVANNI

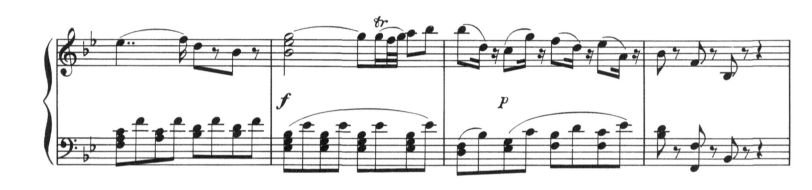

DON OTTAVIO:

Il mio te - so - ro in - tan - to   an -

da - te, an - da - te a con - so - lar,

e del bel ci - glio il pian - to cer - ca - te di a - sciu -

gar,_____ cer - ca - te, cer - ca - te, cer -

ca - te di a - sciu - gar,_____ cer -

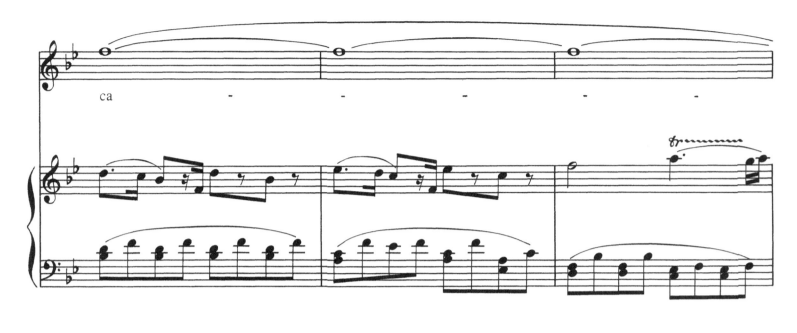

ca - - - - - -

- - te___ di_ a - sciu - gar.

Di - te - le che i suoi tor - ti a ven-di-car io

61

62

nar,   sì,   nun - zio   vo - gl'i - o   tor -

nar!

Il   mio te - so - ro in - tan - to

an - da - te, an - da - te a con - so -

lar,   e del bel ci - gl'io il pian - to cer -

ca - te di a - sciu - gar,   cer - ca - te, cer -

ca - te, cer - ca - te di a - sciu -

64

gar,_____ cer - ca - - - te____ di_ a - sciu - gar.

Di - te - le_ che_i suoi tor - ti a ven-di-car io va - do,

a_ ven-di - car__ i - o va - -

sol di stra - gi e mor - ti

nun - zio vo-gl'io tor - nar, sì,

nun - zio vo-gl'io tor - nar!

Un'aura amorosa

from
COSÌ FAN TUTTE

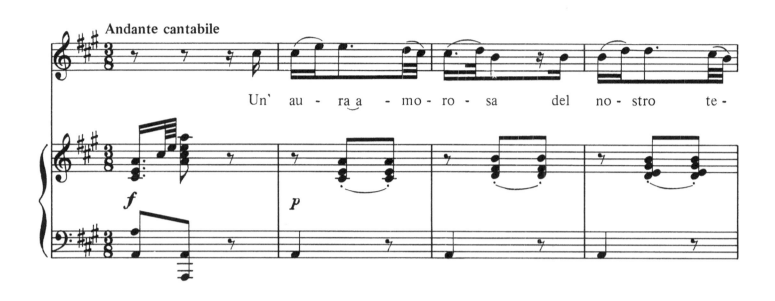

so - ro un dol - ce ri - sto - ro al cor___ por - ge -

rà,_____ un dol - ce ri - sto -

ro al_____ cor por - ge - rà... al

cor che nu - dri - to da spe - me d'a -

no - stro te - so - ro un dol - ce ri - sto - ro al cor___ por-ge-

rà.___ Un' au - ra a - mo - ro - sa del no - stro te - so - ro un

dol - ce ri - sto - ro al cor___ por - ge - rà,___ un dol -

ce ri - sto - ro al___ cor por - ge -

cresc. f p

rà, al__ cor por - ge - rà, al__ cor por - ge -

rà, un dol - ce ri - sto - ro al_ cor____

mf   *p*   *p*   *p*

__ por - ge - rà.

cresc.   *f*

p

Ah! lo veggio quell'anima bella

from
COSÌ FAN TUTTE

Non spe - rar - lo se pria gli oc-chi men fie - ri à me non gi - ri. O

ciel,   ma tu mi guar - di,   e   poi so - spi - ri?

Allegretto

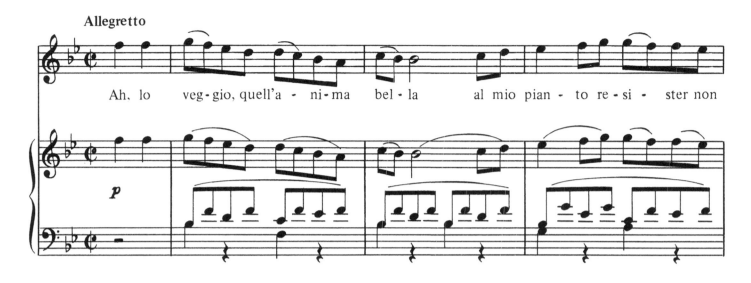

Ah, lo veg - gio, quell'a - ni - ma bel - la al mio pian - to re - si - ster non

sa: non è fat - ta per es - ser ru - bel - la_____ a - gli af -

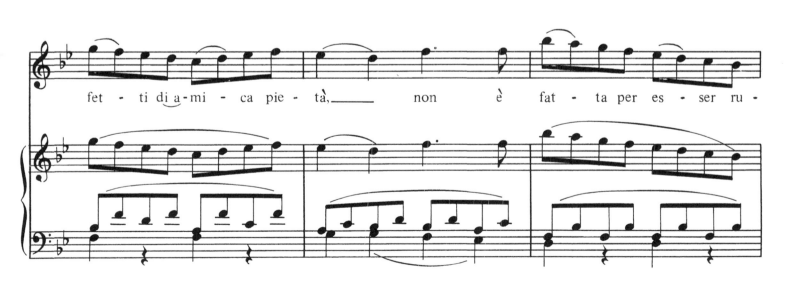

fet - ti di a - mi - ca pie - tà,_____ non è fat - ta per es - ser ru -

bel - la, ru - bel - la a gli af - fet - ti di a - mi - ca pie -

tà. In quel_ guar - do, in quei ca - ri so -

spi - ri dol - ce rag - gio lam - peg - gia al mio cor,_____ lam -

peg - gia al mio cor: già ri - spon-di - a miei cal - di de - si - ri, già tu

te - ne - ro a - mor. Ah, lo veg-gio, quell' a - ni - ma

bel - la al mio pian - to re - si - ster non sa: non è

fat - ta per es - ser ru - bel - la a - gli af - fet - ti di a - mi - ca pie -

tà, non è fat - ta per es - ser ru - bel - la, ru - bel - la a - gli af -

p

fet- - - ti di a - mi - ca pie - tà.

In quel guar - do, in quei ca - ri so - spi - ri dol - ce

rag - gio lam - peg - gia al mio cor,___ lam - peg - gia al mio cor: già ri -

spon - di a miei - cal di de - si - ri, già tu ce - di al più te - ne - ro a -

sa - te, spe - ran - ze fal - la - ci, spe - ran - ze fal-

la - ci, la cru - del_mi con-dan_na_a mor - ir,___ mi con - dan - na a_mo_

rir, la cru - del. Ah ces - sa - te, spe - ran - ze fal-

la - ci, la cru - del_mi con-dan-na a mo - rir,___ la cru - del___ mi con-

dan - na a mo - rir,__ la cru-del__ mi con - dan - na a mo-

rir,__ la cru-del__ mi con-dan - na a mo - rir,__ la cru-del__ mi con-

dan - na, con-dan - na a mo-rir.

Dies Bildnis ist bezaubernd schön

from
DIE ZAUBERFLÖTE

Herz _____ mit neu - er Re - gung _ füllt, mein

Herz _____ mit _ neu - er Re - gung _ füllt.

Dies _ Et - was kann ich zwar nicht

nen - nen; doch _ fühl ich's _ hier wie Feu - er bren - nen.

Soll die Emp-fin - dung__ Lie - be sein? Soll__ die Emp-fin - dung

Lie - be sein? Ja, ja! Die Lie - be ist's al -

lein. Die Lie - be, die Lie - be, die Lie - be

ist's _____ al - lein.

O wenn ich sie nur fin - den könn - te! O wenn sie doch schon vor mir

stän - de! Ich wür - de, wür - de...

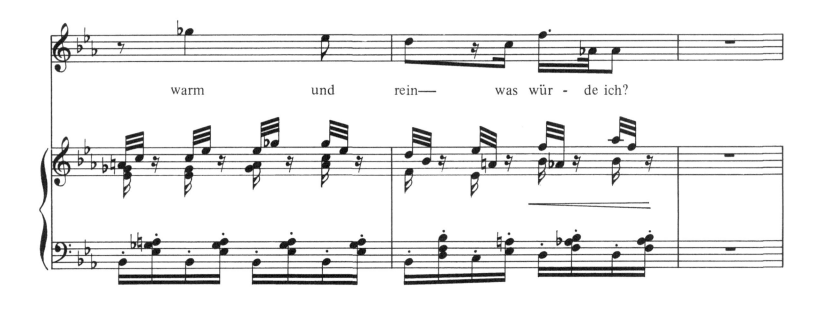

warm und rein— was wür - de ich?

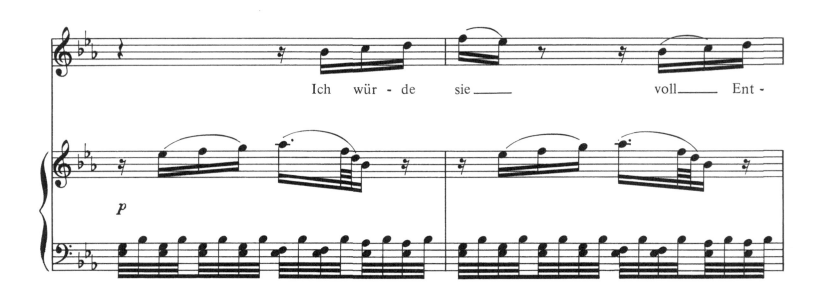

Ich wür - de sie___ voll___ Ent -

zük - ken an die - sen hei - ßen___ Bu - sen___

drück-en, und e-wig wä-re sie dann mein, und e - wig

wä - re sie dann mein, und e - wig wä - re sie dann

mein, e - wig wä - re sie dann mein, e - wig

wä - re sie dann mein.

A series of quality editions for voice from Hal Leonard Publishing.

Classical Carols

concert arrangements by Richard Walters
with a companion CD, including complete
performances with singers,
as well as accompaniments only
00747024 High Voice
00747025 Low Voice

The Classical Singer's Christmas Album

with a companion cassette, including
complete performances with singers on Side A,
accompaniments only on Side B
00747022 High Voice
00747021 Low Voice

Early Puccini for Soprano

Arias from *Le Villi* and *Edgar*
with translations and plot synopses for study
00747028

Puccini:
Two Arias from *La Rondine* for Soprano

with translations and plot synopses for study
00747029

Favorite French Art Songs

with a companion cassette of
the poems recited by a native
French speaker, and piano
accompaniments —
Gary Arvin, pianist;
includes translations and IPA
00312035 High Voice
00312036 Low Voice

Favorite German Art Songs

with a companion cassette of the poems
recited by a native German speaker,
and piano accompaniments—Gary Arvin, pianist;
includes translations and IPA
00312033 High Voice
00312034 Low Voice

Mozart Arias

edited by Robert L. Larsen and Richard Walters
in four volumes, each with a companion
cassette of accompaniments,
Robert L. Larsen, pianist
includes plot synopses and translations for study
(each volume contains ten arias)
00747019 Mozart Arias for Soprano
00747020 Mozart Arias for Mezzo-Soprano
00747018 Mozart Arias for Tenor
00747017 Mozart Arias for Baritone/Bass

Popular Ballads for Classical Singers

songs by Rodgers, Porter, and Gershwin
concert arrangements by Richard Walters
with a companion cassette, including
complete performances with singers on Side A,
accompaniments only on Side B
00660204 High Voice
00660205 Low Voice

Songs of Joseph Marx

with a companion CD of recorded performances
compiled by Gary Arvin; with translations for study
all songs are in the original key
00747027 High Voice
00747026 Medium Voice

Wedding Classics

with a companion cassette, including
complete performances with singers on Side A,
accompaniments only on Side B
00747015 High Voice
00747016 Low Voice

Sacred Classics

with a companion cassette, including
complete performances with singers on Side A,
accompaniments only on Side B
00747013 High Voice
00747014 Low Voice